Ritual

of the

Original Rose

of

Seven Seals

ISBN 1-56459-473-4

Kessinger Publishing's
Rare Mystical Reprints

THOUSANDS OF SCARCE BOOKS ON THESE AND OTHER SUBJECTS:

Freemasonry * Akashic * Alchemy * Alternative Health * Ancient Civilizations * Anthroposophy * Astrology * Astronomy * Aura * Bible Study * Cabalah * Cartomancy * Chakras * Clairvoyance * Comparative Religions * Divination * Druids * Eastern Thought * Egyptology * Esoterism * Essenes * Etheric * ESP * Gnosticism * Great White Brotherhood * Hermetics * Kabalah * Karma * Knights Templar * Kundalini * Magic * Meditation * Mediumship * Mesmerism * Metaphysics * Mithraism * Mystery Schools * Mysticism * Mythology * Numerology * Occultism * Palmistry * Pantheism * Parapsychology * Philosophy * Prosperity * Psychokinesis * Psychology * Pyramids * Qabalah * Reincarnation * Rosicrucian * Sacred Geometry * Secret Rituals * Secret Societies * Spiritism * Symbolism * Tarot * Telepathy * Theosophy * Transcendentalism * Upanishads * Vedanta * Wisdom * Yoga * *Plus Much More!*

DOWNLOAD A FREE CATALOG AT:
www.kessinger.net

OR EMAIL US AT:
books@kessinger.net

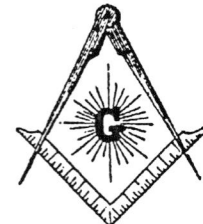

SUPREME OFFICERS

For the

ROSE OF SEVEN SEALS
SUPREME COLLEGE

1—Supreme Most Excellent Rose, north.
2—Supreme Most Excellent Advisor.
3—Supreme Secret Excellent Rose, south.
4—Supreme Select Excellent Rose, west.
5—Supreme Perfect Excellent Rose, east.
6—Supreme Erect Excellent Rose, Secretary.
7—Supreme Honorable Excellent Rose, Treasurer.
8—Supreme Most Wise Excellent Rose, Chaplain.
9—Honorable Secret of Secrets, Inner door.
10—Supreme Honorable Assistance Secret of Secrets, Outer Door.
11—Supreme Princess Excellent Rose, north, right in front.
12—Supreme Worthy Excellent Rose, south, right in front.
13—Supreme Assistant Worthy Excellent Rose, Instruct candidates.
14—Supreme Royal Excellent Rose.

EXTRA NO. 2
OFFICERS, SUBORDINATE COLLEGE
ROSE OF SEVEN SEALS

1—Most Excellent Rose, north.
2—Most Excellent Advisor.
3—Secret Excellent Rose, south.
4—Select Excellent Rose, west.
5—Perfect Excellent Rose, east.
6—Erect Excellent Rose, Secretary.
7—Honorable Excellent Rose, Treasurer.
8—Most Wise Excellent Rose, Chaplain.
9—Honorable Secret of Secrets, Inner Door.
10—Assistant Secret of Secrets, Outer Door.
11—Princess Excellent Rose, north right front.
12—Worthy Excellent Rose, South right front.
13—Assistant Worthy Excellent Rose.
14—Royal Excellent Rose.

QUORUM:

Seven members constitute a quorum. Election to be held on or before the 3rd of December each year. The legal representative to all Supreme Rose of Seven Seals are the first seven officers, four at the will of the Subordinate College.

OPENING CEREMONY

Seven raps call the council together. The Princess Excellent Rose lays the bible on the altar open at the 6th chapter of Rev. and places 7 candles on the most excellent station north, and the select station in the west 2, and the Secret Station in the south 4, and the perfect Station in the east 1.

The Book of Constitution at the Erect Excellent Station, Ritual on each of the four stations.

The Most Excellent two raps with the gavel. The Perfect Excellent makes two raps with the gavel, calling all members to their feet, each making due guard sign of the Rose of Seven Seals.

(The Most Excellent to the Secret Excellent): You will carefully examine each and collect the pass word.

(Secret Excellent): I see. I feel we are secure. Permit me to make a speedy inspection, Most Excellent.

(Most Excellent): You may and report your findings.

(Secret Excellent to Select Excellent): Carefully examine your Rose, and secure the pass from each.

(Select Excellent collects the pass from all in her avenue, and reports her findings to the Secret Excellent, and Secret Excellent reports to Most Excellent).

(Secret to Most Excellent): All present have the pass except those you see standing.

(The Most Excellent will advise the Secret Excellent the course of procedure to take.)

(Secret Excellent to Most Excellent): Your orders have been obeyed, and we are secure.

(Most Excellent officers and members of the College, we have been assured by the Secret Excellent

Rose and her assistants that we are secure and by the high power and authority invested in me, I, _____declare the College duly opened. Most Wise Excellent Rose, perform your duty.

(The Wise Rose) will read a verse of the 6th chapter of Revelations, sing a song and prayer. When this is completed, the most Excellent Rose will make the due guard sign and announce that the College is open for business.

The Secret Excellent Rose will report to the Select Excellent Rose, the Select Excellent Rose, the Perfect Excellent and the Perfect Excellent reports to members: Officers and members of the Seven Seals, the word has come down the line to me that this College is open for business, you will take due notice and govern yourselves accordingly. For it is the will and pleasure of the Most Excellent Rose, and I ask all officers and members take their respective stations. Erect Excellent, kindly call the roll of officers, read the minutes of your last meeting, perform your duty in general.

Most Excellent, your orders have been obeyed, officers have been instructed.

(Most Excellent to Erect Excellent): I thank you Erect Excellent. You shall be long remembered for your faithful service, your support in this College work.

ORDER OF BUSINESS.

Erect Excellent proceeds to read the minutes of last meeting, after this, the Most Excellent calls for roll of officers, and new business, unfinished business, collection of dues and assessments, receiving and referring of petitions and making of donations. Committees report:

(Most Excellent to Princess Excellent): You will inspect the outer Chamber of the College to ascertain if there are any candidates waiting for reception. If so, you will kindly report the name of person, name of court or lodge and number from whence they hail. Should you need any assistance, the Worthy Excellent Rose will accompany you, to prepare the candidates. When the candidates are prepared, the Princess Excellent will alarm the door with three raps, the Honorable Secret of Secrets will answer with four raps, and reply, Who is this that alarms our college?

(Princess Excellent Answers): It is one who comes all the way from the Royal house of the Courts, the Home of the Sphinx, and desires to enter admission here with us.

(The Inside Guard): Has she been vouched for?
Answer: She has.
Question: Is she qualified?
Answer: She is. Let her wait with patience until the Most Excellent is informed of this request.

The Honorable Secret of Secrets report to the Most Excellent that the candidate has met all qualifications and is prepared for the reception.

(Most Excellent to the Honorable Secret of Secrets): You will make the necessary inspection. If she is willing to submit, then you may admit her.

(Honorable Secret of Secrets returns to the door), makes four raps on the door and says to the candidate, is this your own voluntary petition? that you seek admission here with us?

Candidate answers: Yes, it is.
Honorable, is it your intention to submit to our laws, rules and regulations?
It is.
Is it your intention to be good and true and support this College work to the best of your ability?
It is.
Since you have consented to become united with us, I will instruct the Princess Excellent to carry you through the halls of science, into the chambers of

culture where the door will open wide to every delightful inquirer. The place where the truth will be fully explained. I shall leave you here alone with the Princess Excellent and when you hear the sound of the gavel, you will proceed on your journey with us.

(The Honorable Secret of Secrets returns and makes the report approving the candidate). The Most Excellent sounds the gavel four times, the door is opened, the Princess Excellent enters with the candidate, she is led to the station in the west, while all the members continue singing ... _____, where the first seal is read, then to the east where the second and third seals are read, to the south where the fourth and fifth seals are read, to the north where the 6th and 7th Seals are read, then the Most Excellent rises and makes the following address:

Friends, you stand before us seeking admission into this College, we trust that your motives are good, that your hearts are true and that it is your intention to look to the great light of reason, to the gracious Being above, and to follow in full submission where ever his will may lead. We do pray that your solemn engagement and the work of today will be long remembered by you; we further pray that our ceremonies will be of much benefit to you, a lesson that you may learn in this college will serve to lift a fallen race and prove beneficial to the future generation yet unborn. We note in your petition that you have traveled through the royal roads and many scenes and journeys to this College.

Beware, my friends, ever remember we bear each other's burdens, we share each others sorrows, we share each others joy and happiness, we look to the bright side of life, we attempt to send a ray of sunshine through every home, to make each happy, we visit the sick, we keep a watchful eye over the widows and orphans, we honor the sublime Prince of the Royal Secret, and the Illustrious Inspectors General of the A. A. S. Rite, 33rd, we stand ready at all times to defend their cause, we support our Most Puissant Sovereign Grand Commander, for under his watchful care we are surely protected. His hand sways over a destiny of a great nation. I cannot invoke for you any greater success than that of a homely virtue who sold his truth. So go younder my sister where you have traveled before, stand this trial, stand this test and when you have been placed at the Altar on both knees, I do pray that the Great God, the ruler of the human destiny will have mercy on you. You may pray in silence, and when yo have finished you may raise your right hand.

(Candidate is carried through a rough and rugged road until she reaches the Altar, she is told to fall upon her knees, and to pray for herself, finally, when her hand is raised, she is brought back to the Most Secret Excellent Station where she is given the bread of life.) This is a small piece of bitter apple). She is taken to the next station where she is pitied, they tell her to take a drink that she may not taste of such and longer. (But this drink is a little warm water with a little Epsom salts in it). She is carried to the next station, this being the most Excellent Station, she is told to kiss the Seven Seals to show that she will never reveal what transpired in the College. But this seal is that of one pod of red pepper. At the close of this seal, she is sent to the altar to take an obligtaion. On the Altar rest the Holy Bible opened on the 6th chapter of Revelation, with seven candles burning, and incense. And she contracts the following obligations:

I,_____, in the presence of the

witnesses around me, do promise to adhere to the principles of the College and its teachings, to obey its laws, rules and regulations. I further promise never to reveal the secrets of this work unless he or she is lawfully entitled as I am myself. I further promise to stand by the Sublime Prince of the Royal Secrets and the Inspector General, 33rd, and last degree. I promise to visit the Colllege which I may be a member of, and I will visit the sick and contribute as freely as possible. All this I most solemnly declare so help me God. (She kisses the Seal). (The candidate is uncovered, she discovers the seven candles burning, she sees the incense burning and on each of the four station she discovers the candles burning. Total number of candles burning at that time is fourteen.) (She is told to look to the north, she is saluted by the Most Excellent who gives her the signs, being assisted by the Secret Excellent and Select Excellent.

SIGN AND WORD OF THE ROSE

Place your left hand on the left side of your head, fingers closed and looking down. The word is, I see. The answer is made by the right hand resting on the right hip, four fingers closed, thumb in a perpendicular position. The word is: I have.

OBLIGATION OF THE ROSE OF SEVEN SEALS

I, A. B., of my own free will and accord, in the presence of the Almighty God and the witnesses around me, do hereby solemnly promise as I have heretofore done with this additional, that I will not speak evil against my sister or brother; but will strive to keep peace and harmony within the ranks, and I will not violate any laws, rules or regulations of the Ancient Accepted Scottish Rite but will answer to all summons and obey all proclamations handed to me, it coming from the legal and lawful authority. I further promise that I will never give my consent to making of any unworthy character nor to any person who is not lawfully entitled to receive this degree.

I further promise to support the United Supreme Council of the Ancient Accepted Scottish Rite Masons and this College work whenever I am called on and defend its cause, to contribute when I can do so without material injury to myself, to support our Most Puissant Sovereign Grand Commander, Our Supreme Most Excellent Rose whenever called upon, all of this I solemnly promise without the least evasion, so help me God, and keep me steadfast, this my solemn obligation. Amen. Amen. Amen. Amen.

SIGN AND WORK

Candidate looking to the north, she discovers the Most Excellent with her right foot crossed over left, with thumb of the hand under the left eye, the index curved over the left eye. The word is: I know. Ans.: I will, made by the Most Select Rose, with her left foot over her right, with her right thumb under the right eye, the index finger curved above.

DIALOGUE

Most Excellent to Select Excellent—Are you a Rose?
Select Excellent—I have viewed the Seals.
Most Excellent—I see the Seven.
Select Excellent—I know where the roses bloom, can you tell me.
Most Excellent—I will with your assistance.
Select Excellent—C O L.
Most Excellent—L E G E. They both spell College.
Select Excellent: You are a Princess.

Most Excellent—I am first among my equals, I have stood the test.

Select Excellent—Then you are a Princess, from Jerusalem.

Most Excellent—I have borne the burden, I have loosed the slaves, I have freed the nation.

HAND-SHAKE.

Join the index finger of the right hand, the first make four taps with the thumb on the hand, the second makes three taps, the first says Rose, the second say Seven, both say Seals.

DUTY OF OFFICERS

1. Most Excellent Rose is the presiding officer.
2. Most Excellent Advisor: Must be a member of a Consistory in good and regular standing with the Supreme Council. His duty is to act as advisor to the Most Excellent Rose and the College.
3. Secret Excellent Rose is the second officer.
4. Select Excellent Rose, third officer.
5. Perfect Excellent Rose, fourth officer.
6. Erect Excellent Rose, secretary.
7. Honorable Excellent Rose, treasurer.
8. Most Wise Excellent Rose, Chaplain.
9. Honorable Secret of Secrets, Inner Door.
10. Assistant Secret of Secrets, Outer Door.
11. Princess Excellent Rose, attendant of the Most Excellent Rose.
12. Worthy Excellent Rose, attendant of Secret Excellent Rose.
13. Assistant Worthy Excellent Rose, attendant on Select Excellent Rose.
14. Royal Excellent Rose, attendant on Perfect Excellent Rose.

CLOSING CEREMONIES.

The Business of the College having been completed the Most Excellent Rose Proceeds as follows:

M. Ex Rose. does any work or benevolence remain unperformed?

Secret Ex Rose: None, that I recall M. Ex. Rose.

M. Ex Rose; Then Hon. S. of S. (inner door keeper) you will instruct them that we are about to close this College and to permit no disturbance to be made; until the M. Wise Excellent Rose have invoked God's blessings upon us.

S. of S. No disturbance will be made M. Ex. Rose.

(PRAYER BY Most Wise Excellent Rose.)

M. Ex Rose. Officers and members of the College of the Rose of Seven Seals; We will join hands as we sing our closing ode; (God Be With You Till we meet again;)

M. Ex. Rose; Sisters and brothers as we part let us set a standard, according to our obligations that is standing for Christ and his cause, knowing that our heavenly Father will watch over us and give us strength to go forward and hold us by his power.

Prayer in Unison: (Eternal Father help us to seek the friendship of Jesus Christ as the first concern of our lives; and when day is done and the crown of life is won.)

May we hear your welcome Voice Saying

"WELL DONE"

AMEN.   AMEN.   AMEN.   AMEN.

The following mystical pictures are not related to this book.

They have been included for your enjoyment.

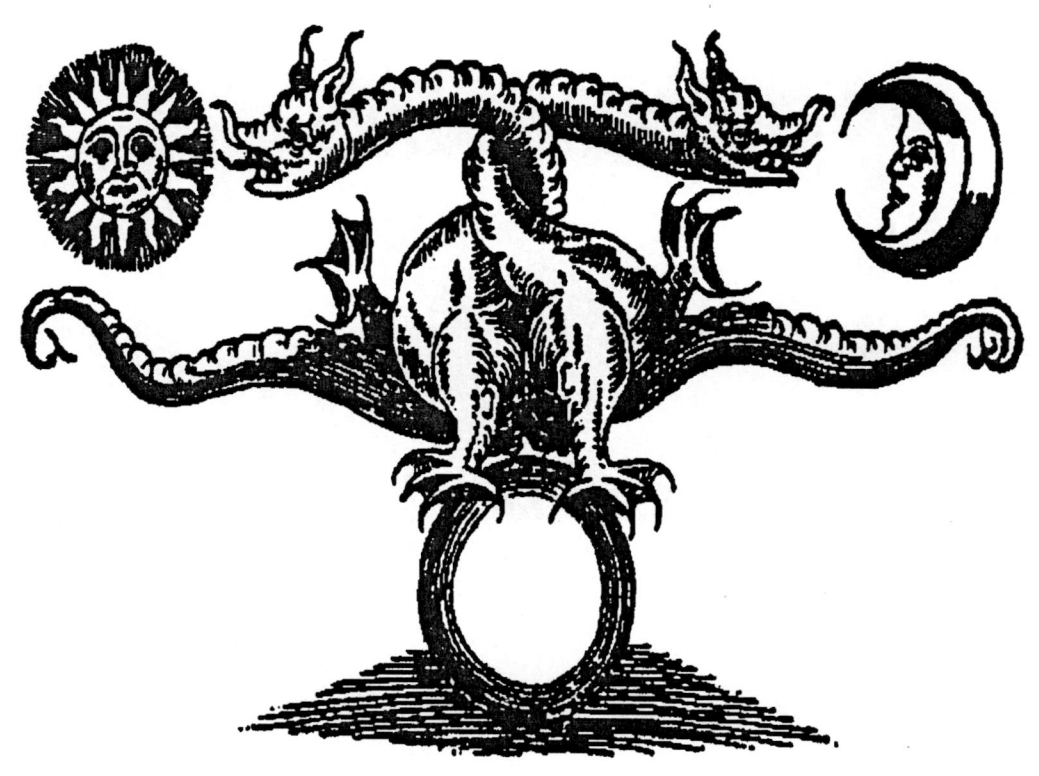

Pictures 1

Pictures 2

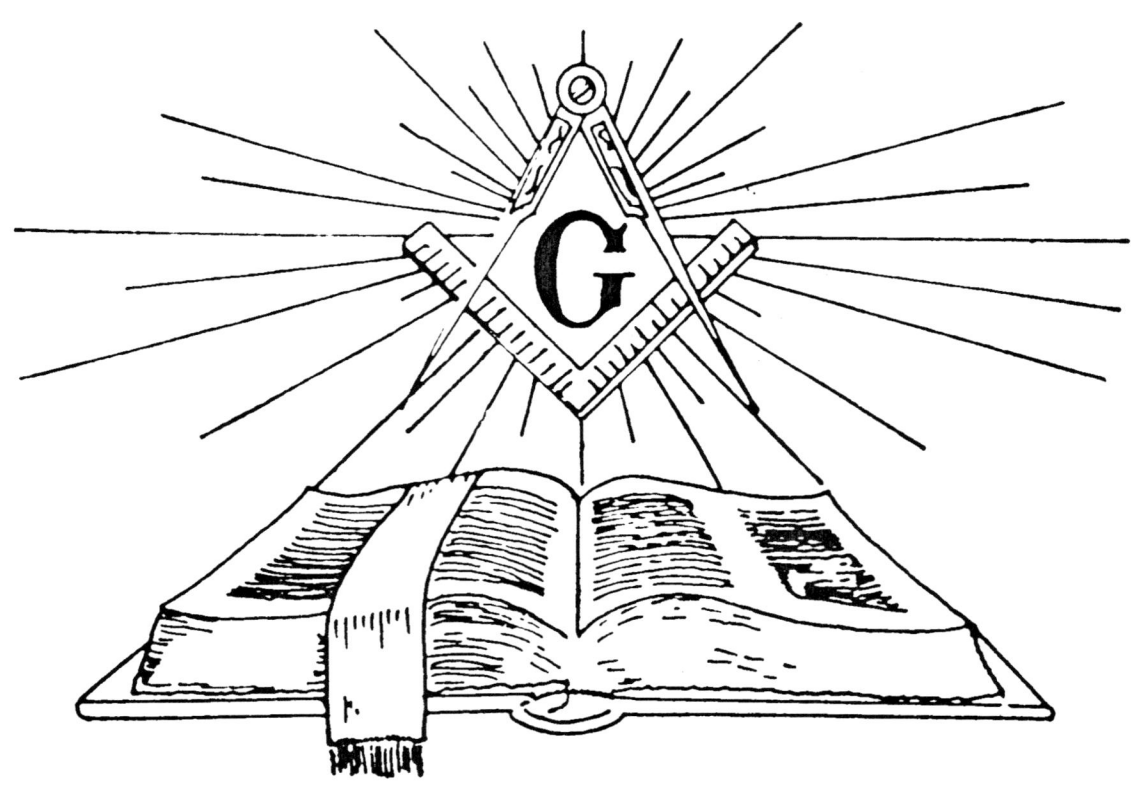

Pictures 5

ALCHYMIA
(From Thurneysser's Quinta Essentia, 1570)

Pictures 6

Pictures 7

Pictures 8

Pictures 9

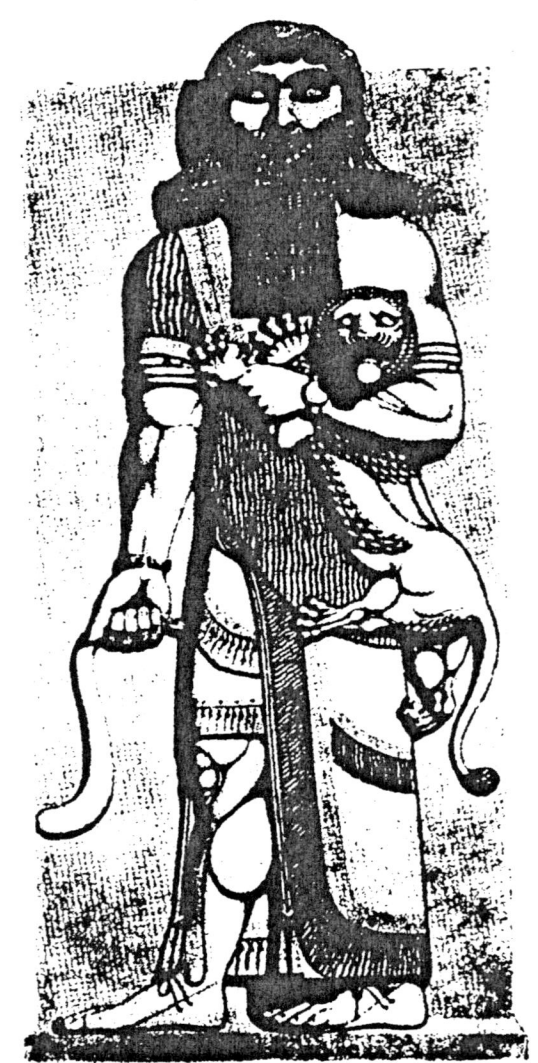

Assyrian Type of Gilgamesh

Pictures 11

MASONIC APRON PRESENTED TO GEN. WASHINGTON
BY MADAME LAFAYETTE.

THE GOLDEN WHEEL

Pictures 15

Pictures 16

Pictures 17

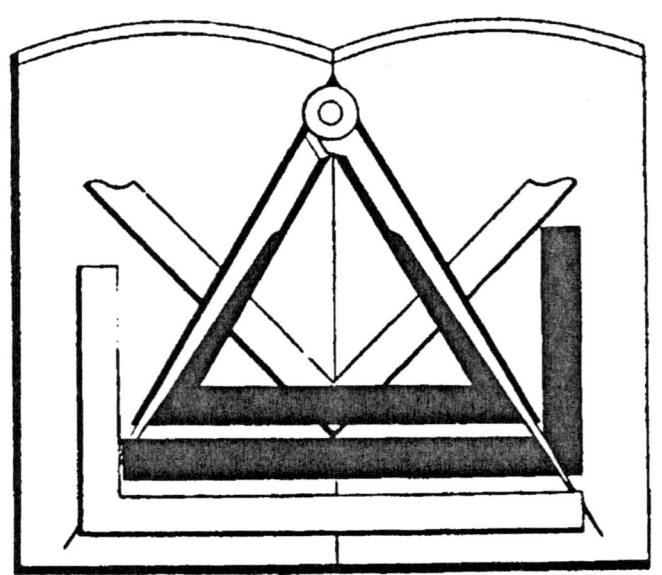

Pictures 18

Pictures 19

Pictures 20

Pictures 21

Pictures 22

Pictures 23

Pictures 24

Pictures 25

MERCURIUS DE MERCURIO

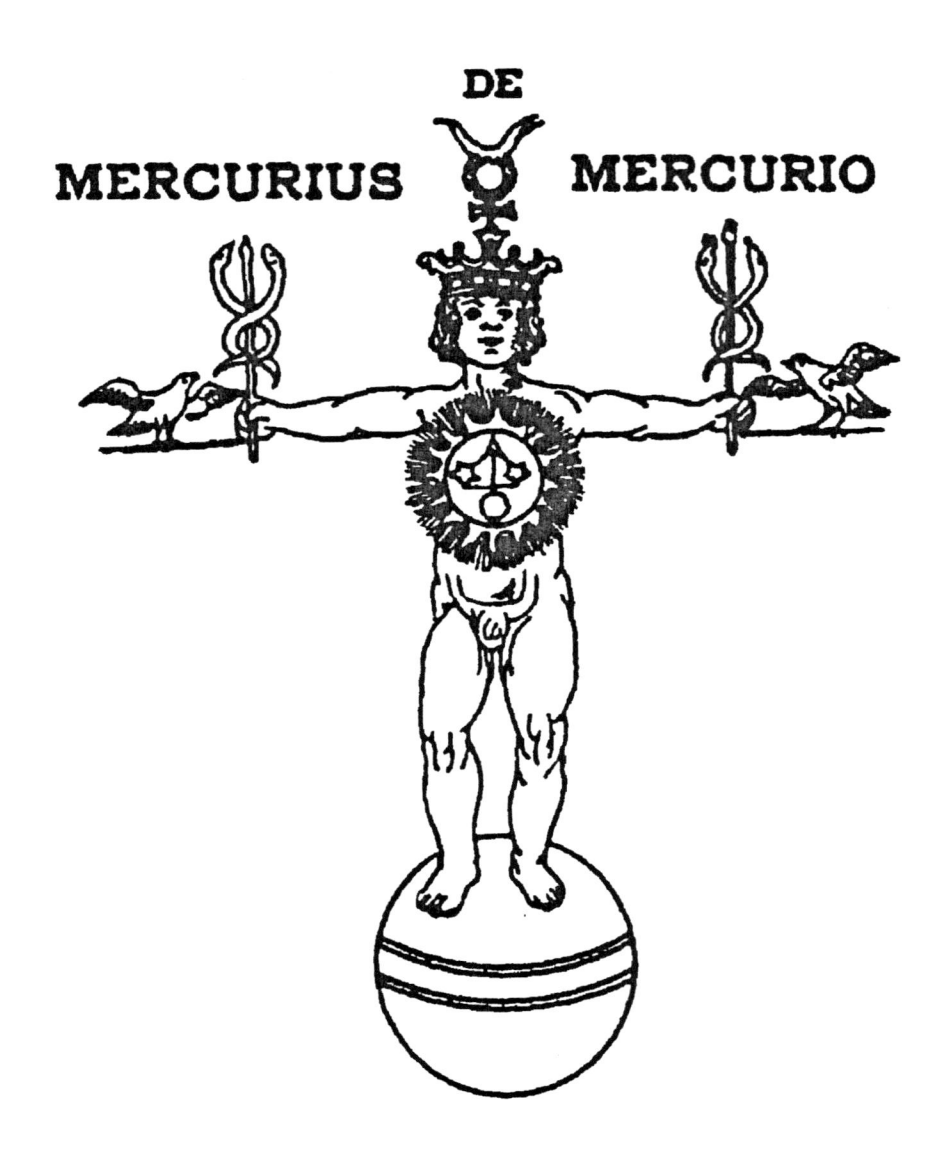

Pictures 27

Pictures 28

Pictures 29

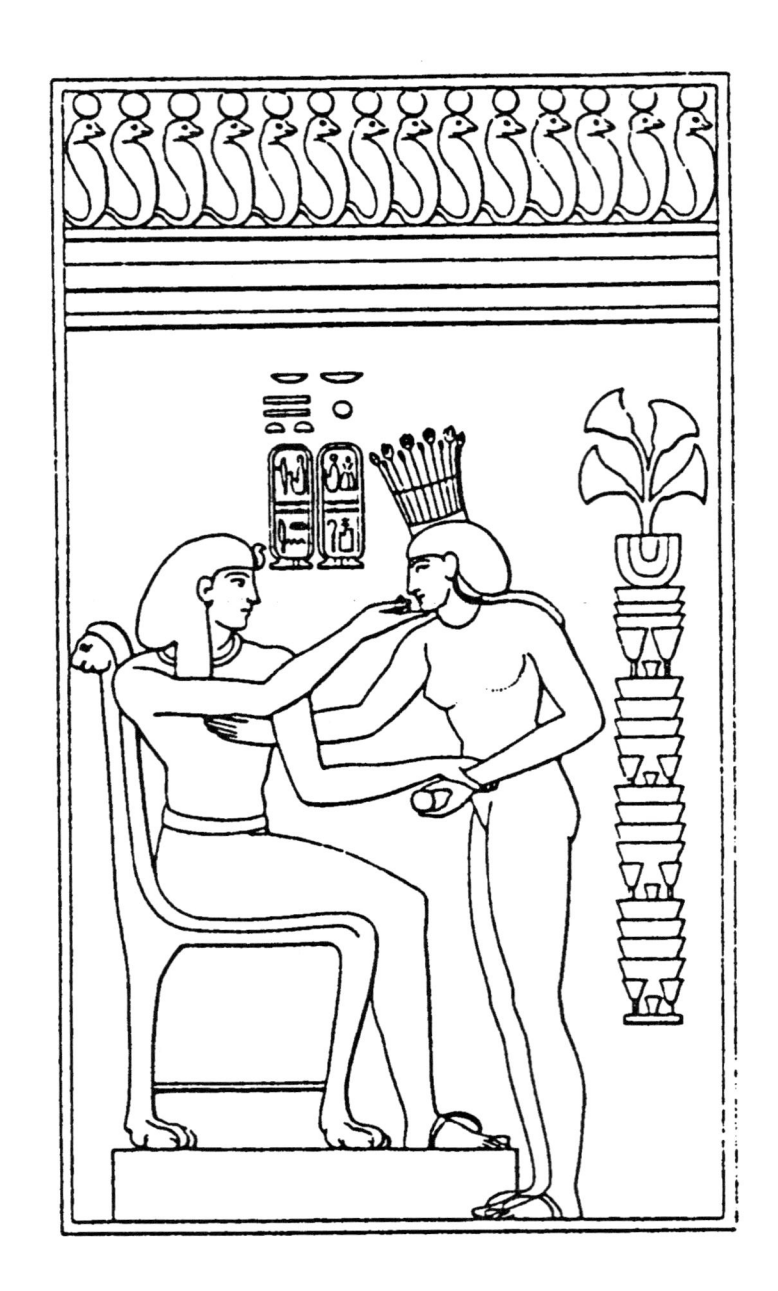

Pictures 30

Pictures 31

Pictures 32

Pictures 33

Pictures 34

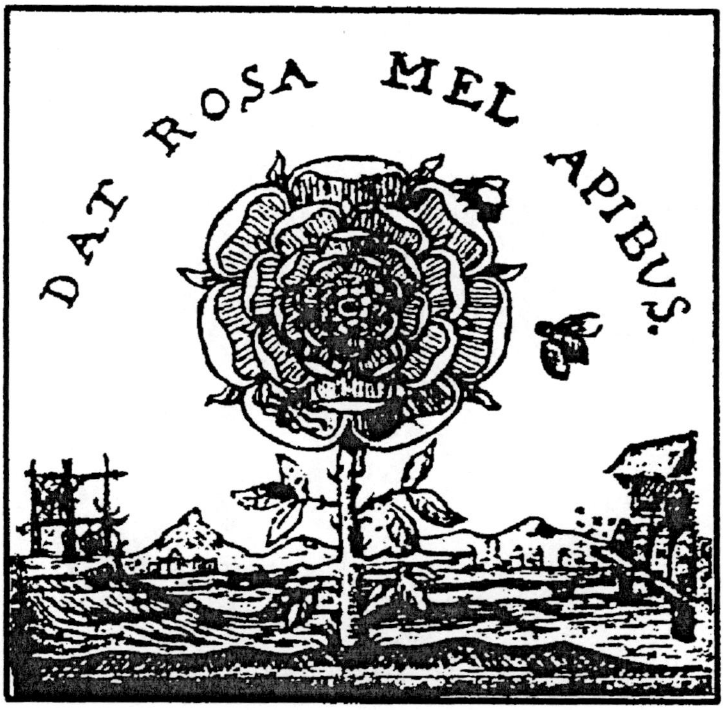
DAT ROSA MEL APIBUS.

Pictures 36

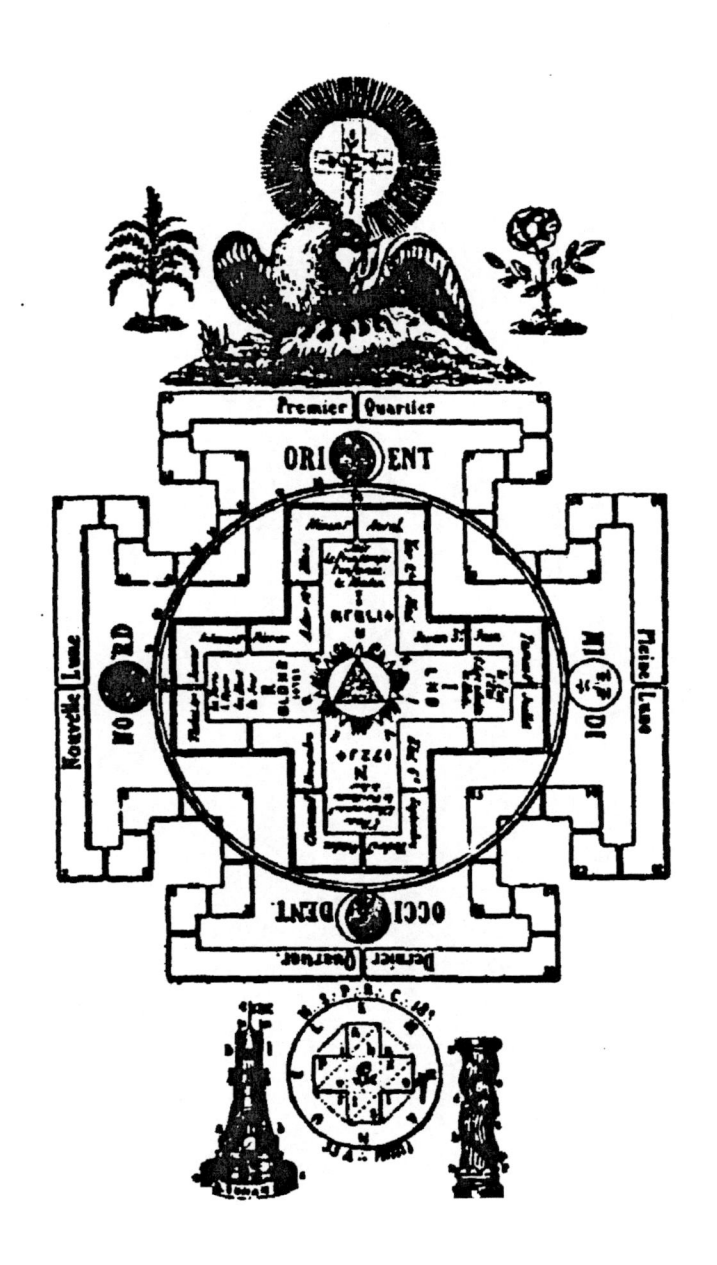

Pictures 37

ADDA-NARI

Pictures 38

Pictures 39

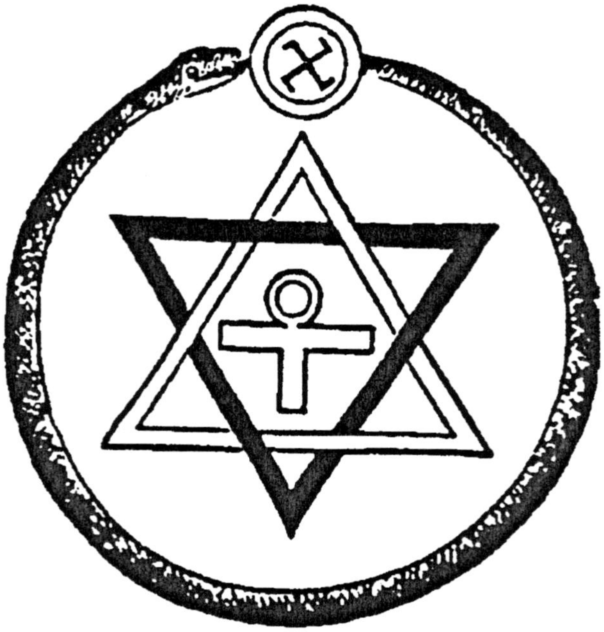

Pictures 40

Pictures 41

Pictures 42

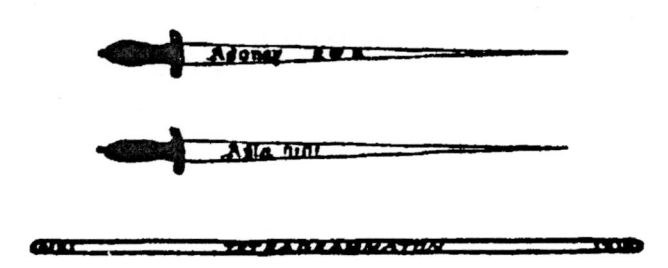

THE MAGIC CIRCLE AND WEAPONS.

Pictures 43

Pictures 44

Pictures 45

Pictures 46

Pictures 47

Pictures 48

Pictures 49

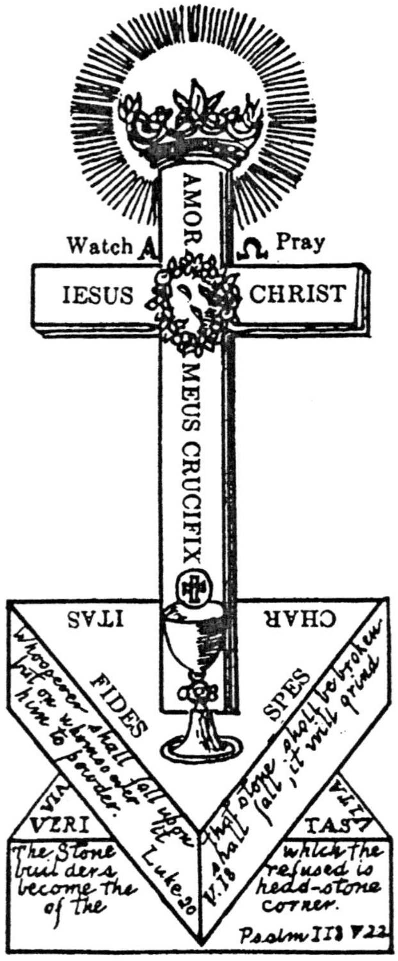
AMOR
Watch
Pray
IESUS
CHRIST
MEUS CRUCIFIX
CHAR
ITAS
FIDES
SPES
VIA
VERI
TAS
VITA
The Stone which the builders refused is become the head-stone of the corner.
Psalm 118 V 22
Whosoever shall fall upon that stone shall be broken
Luke 20 V. 18

Pictures 51

Pictures 52

Pictures 53

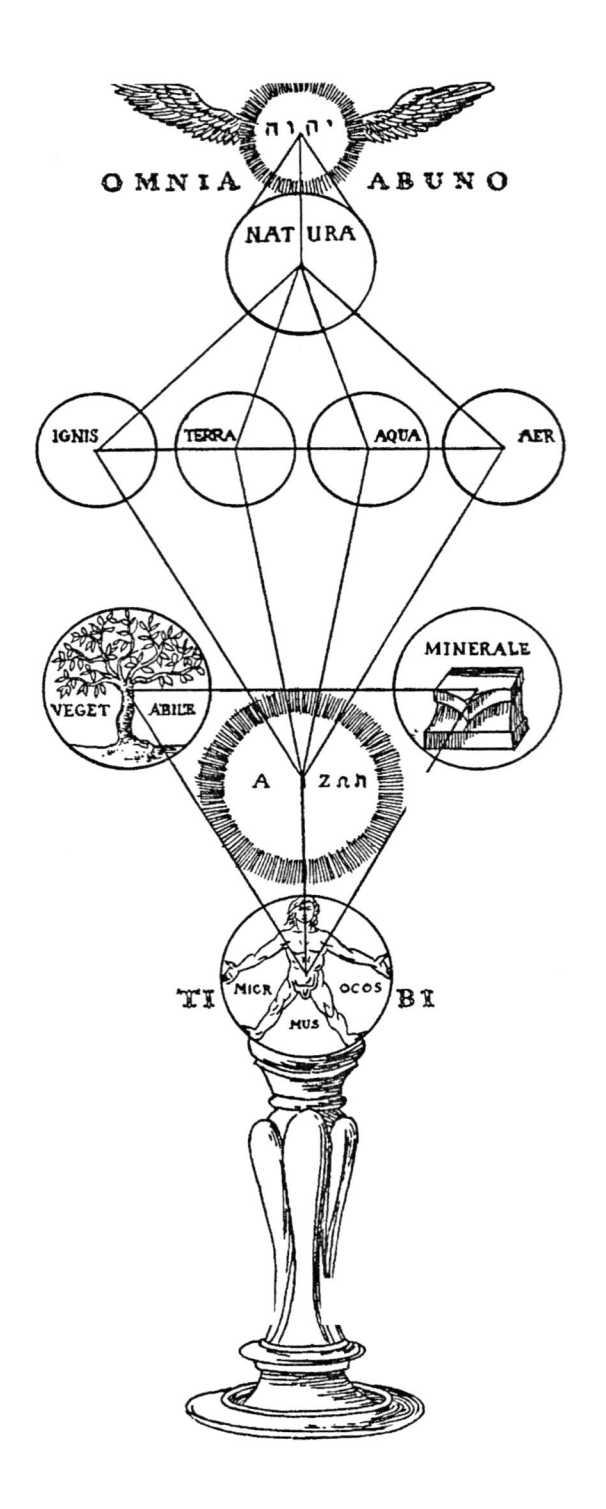

Pictures 54

Pictures 55

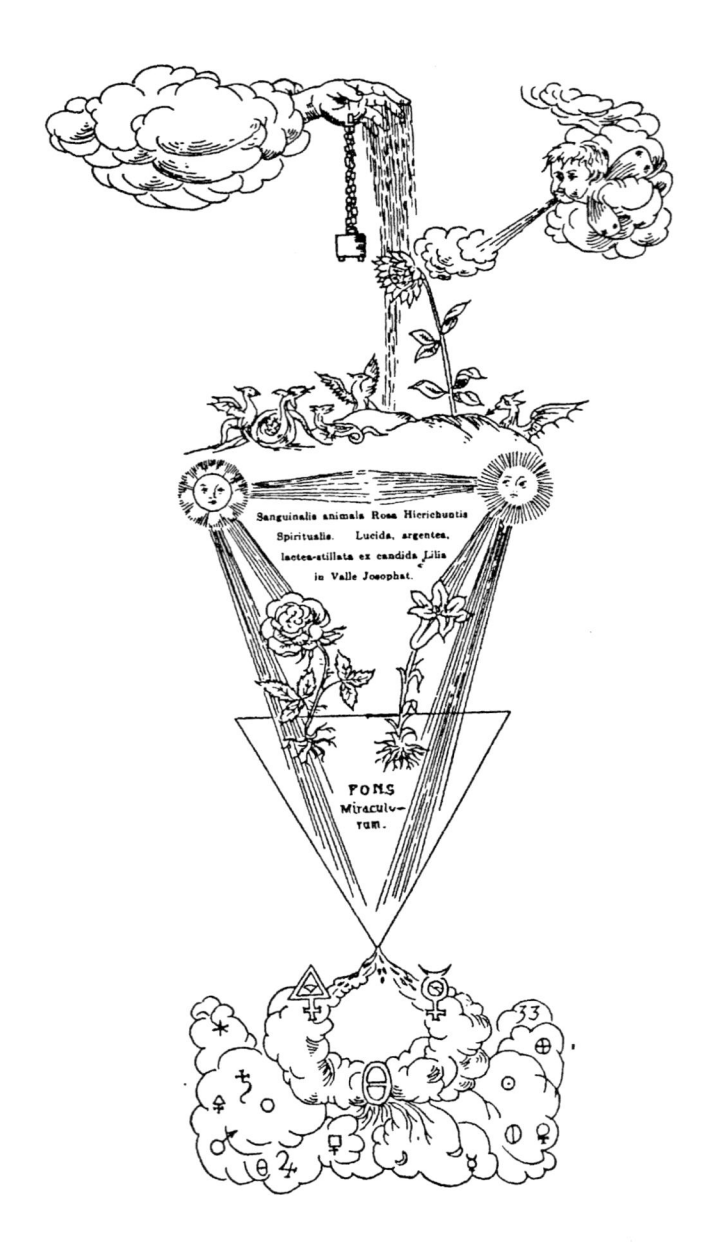

Sanguinalis animalis Rosa Hierichuntis
Spiritualis. Lucida, argentea,
lactea-stillata ex candida Lilia
in Valle Josophat.

PONS
Miraculu-
rum.

Pictures 56

Pictures 57

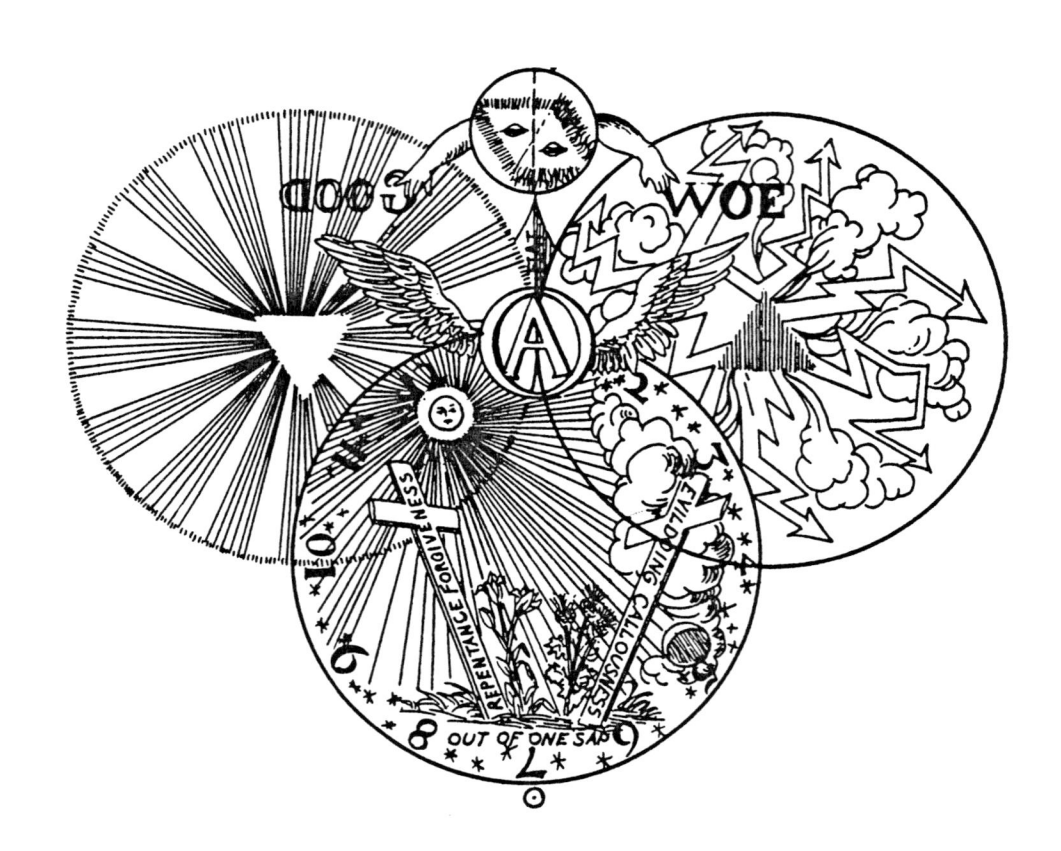

Pictures 58

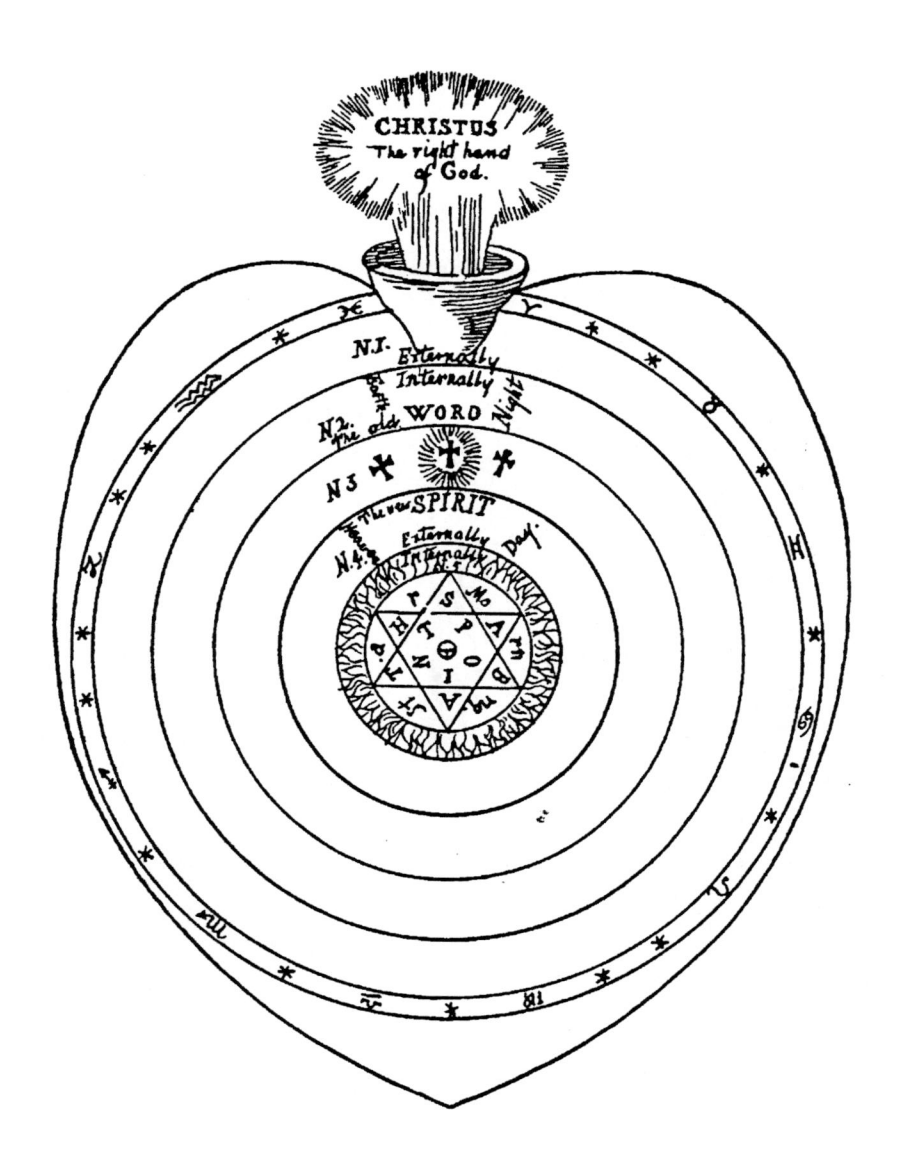

Pictures 59

Pictures 60

Pictures 61

Spiritus, Anima, Corpus.

Pictures 63

Pictures 64

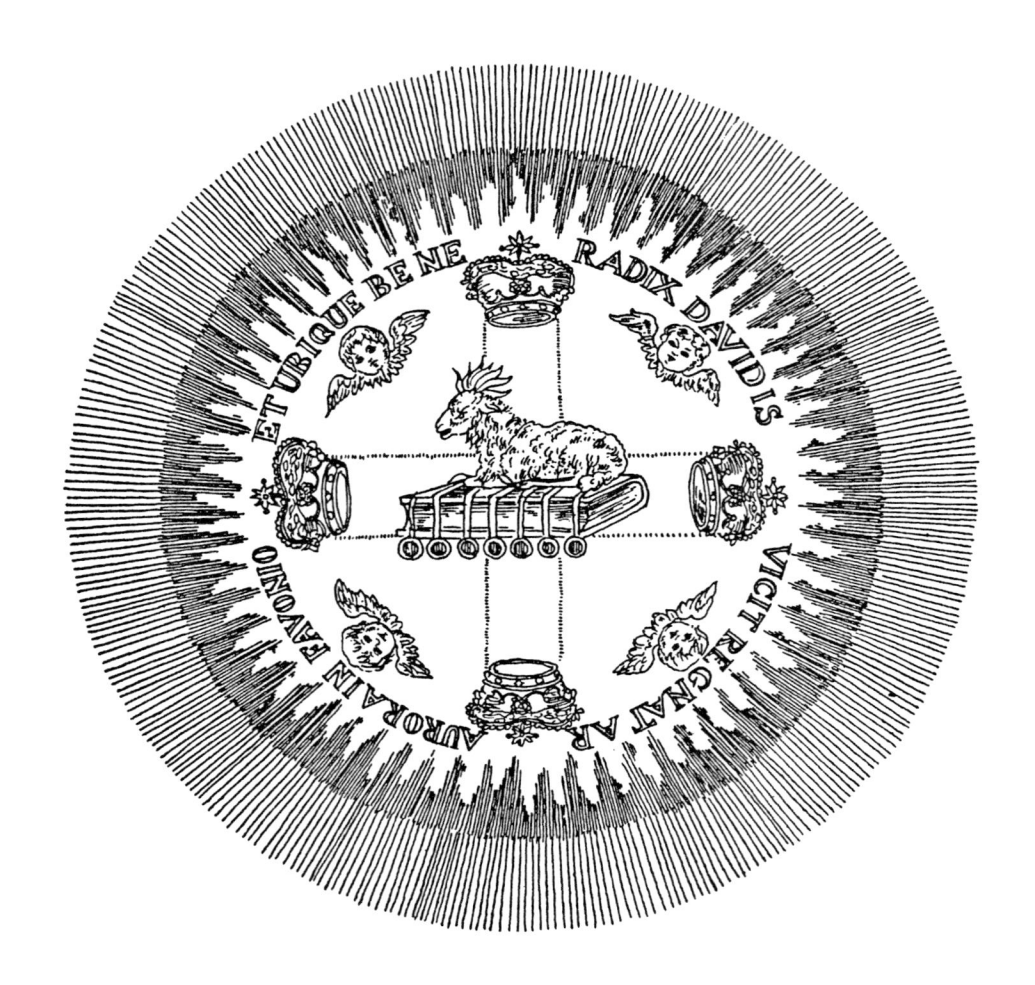

Pictures 65

Pictures 66

Pictures 67

THE GOLDEN WHEEL

VISITA INTERIORA TERRÆ RECTIFICANDO INVENIES OCCULTUM LAPIDEM

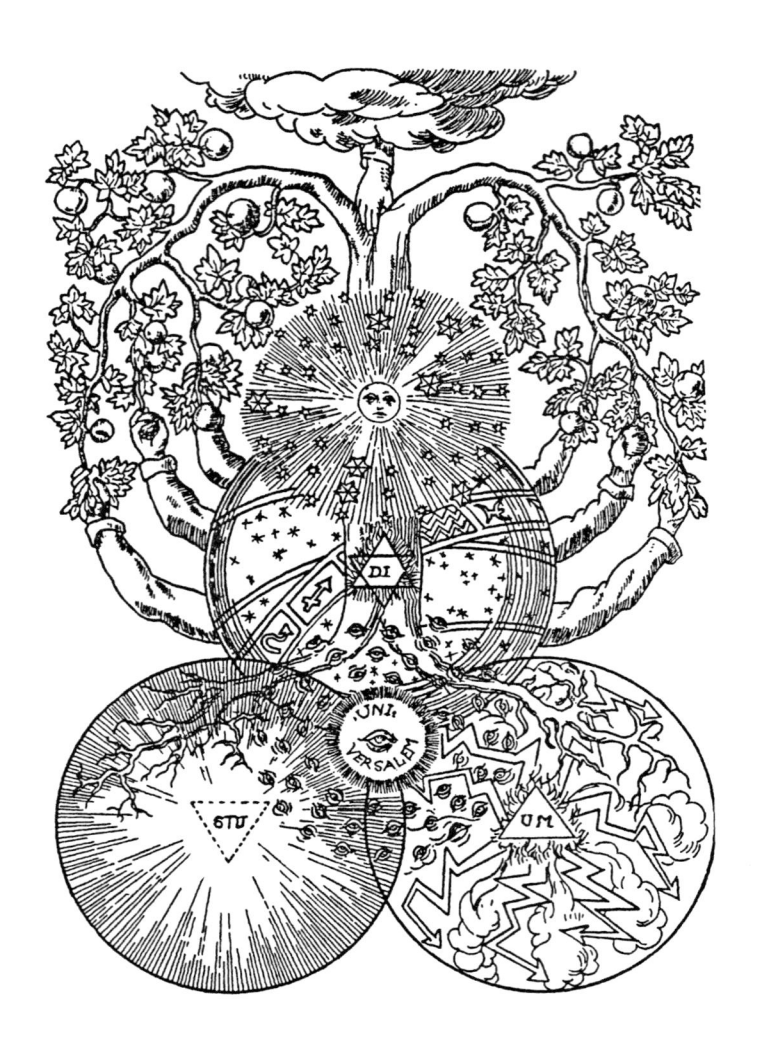

Pictures 70

Pictures 71

Pictures 72

Pictures 73

Pictures 74

Pictures 75

Pictures 76

Pictures 77

Pictures 78

Pictures 79

Pictures 80

Pictures 81

Pictures 82

Pictures 83

PSALM. 133.

Pictures 85

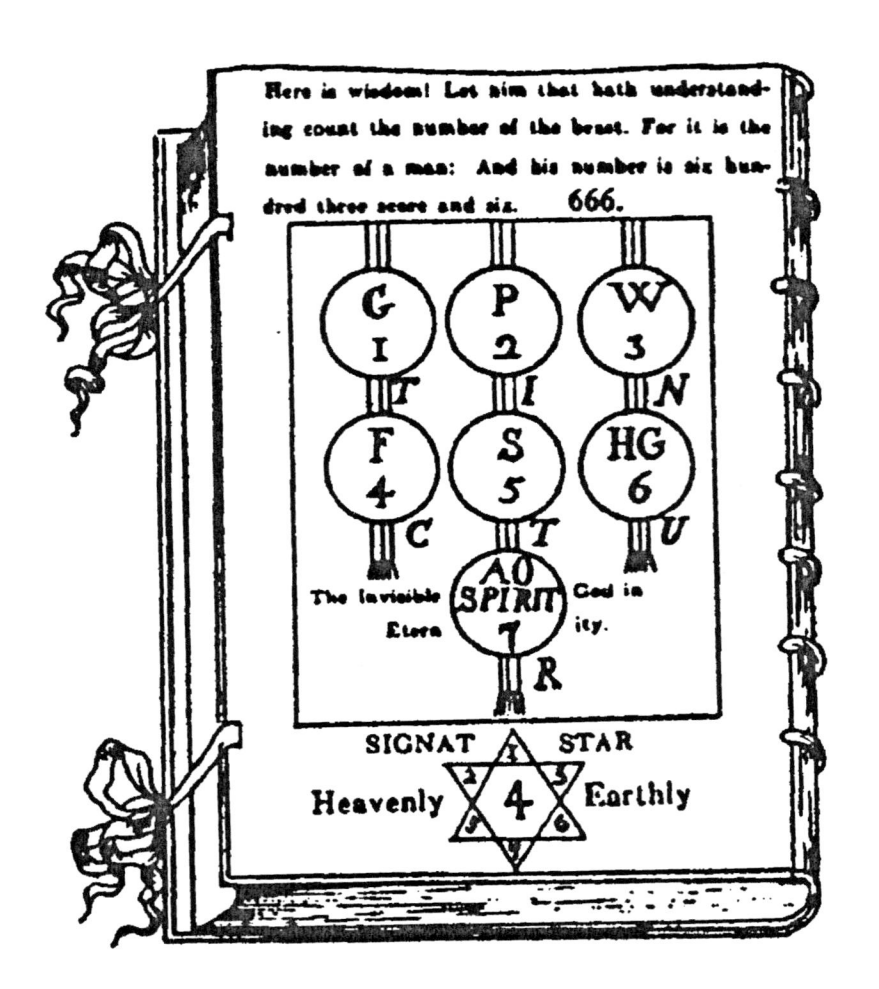

Here is wisdom! Let him that hath understanding count the number of the beast. For it is the number of a man: And his number is six hundred three score and six. 666.

- G / I / IT
- P / 2 / I
- W / 3 / N
- F / 4 / C
- S / 5 / T
- HG / 6 / U
- AO / SPIRIT / 7 / R

The Invisible Eternal God in ity.

SIGNAT STAR

Heavenly 4 Earthly

Pictures 87

Pictures 88

Pictures 89

Pictures 90

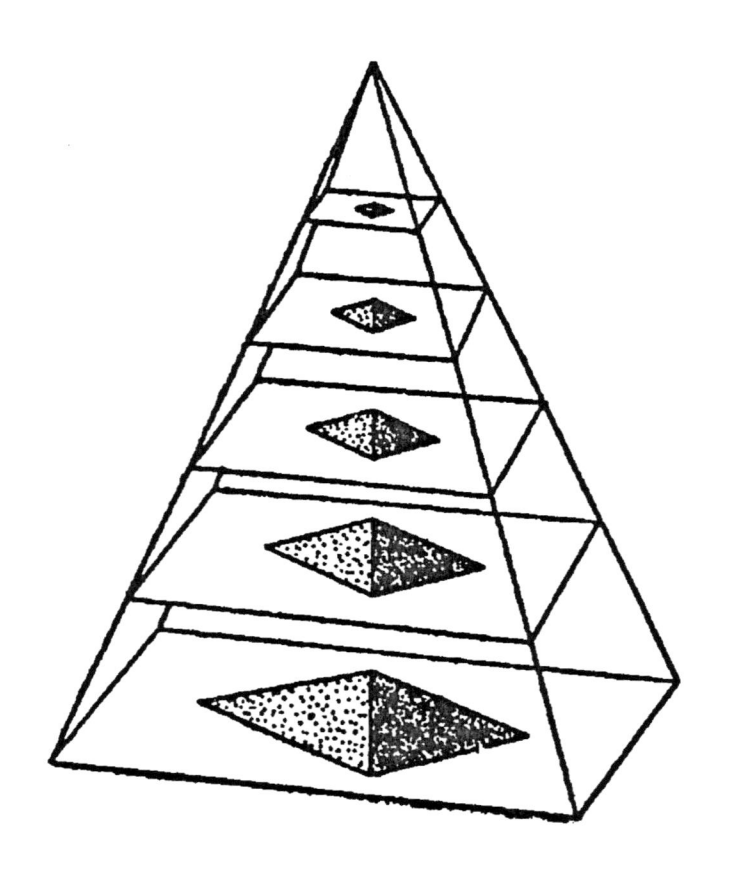

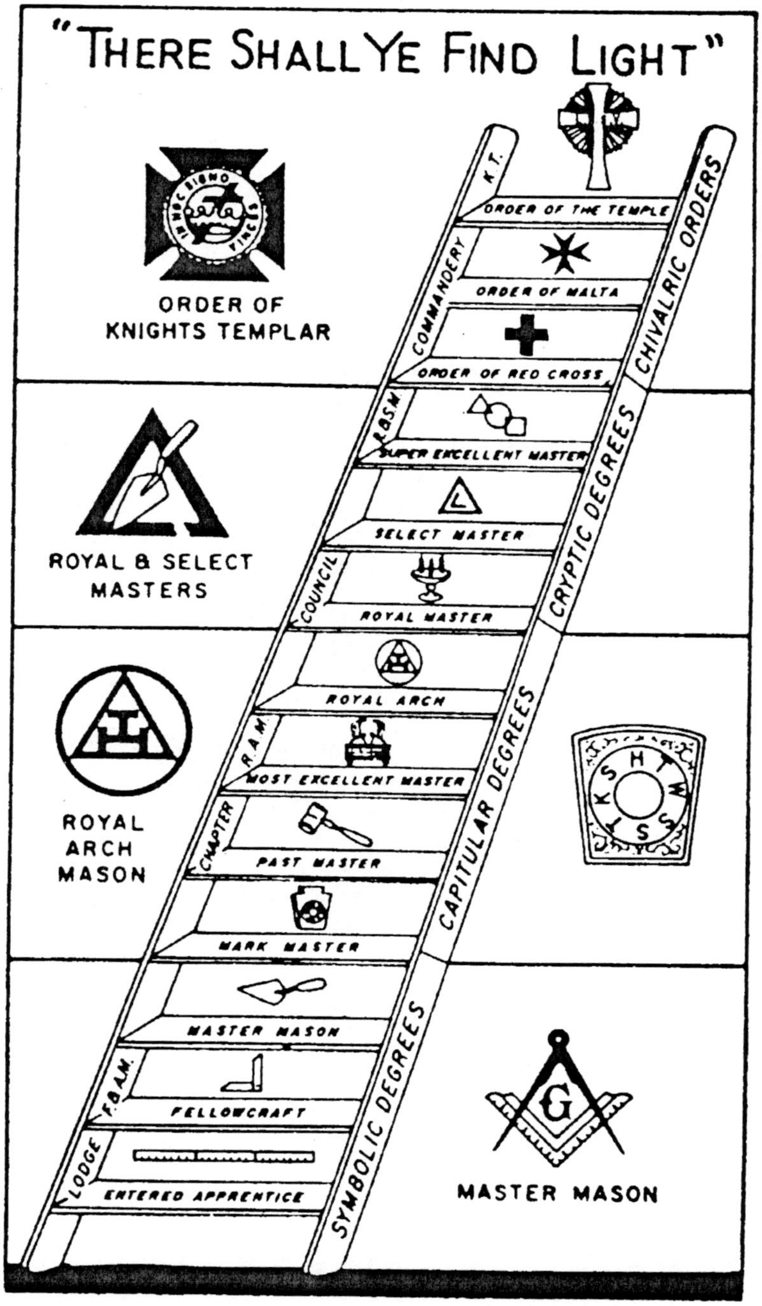
"THERE SHALL YE FIND LIGHT"
ORDER OF KNIGHTS TEMPLAR
ROYAL & SELECT MASTERS
ROYAL ARCH MASON
MASTER MASON
K.T.
ORDER OF THE TEMPLE
COMMANDERY
ORDER OF MALTA
ORDER OF RED CROSS
R.&S.M.
SUPER EXCELLENT MASTER
SELECT MASTER
COUNCIL
ROYAL MASTER
ROYAL ARCH
R.A.M.
MOST EXCELLENT MASTER
CHAPTER
PAST MASTER
MARK MASTER
MASTER MASON
F.&A.M.
FELLOWCRAFT
LODGE
ENTERED APPRENTICE
CHIVALRIC ORDERS
CRYPTIC DEGREES
CAPITULAR DEGREES
SYMBOLIC DEGREES
G

Pictures 92

Printed in the United Kingdom
by Lightning Source UK Ltd.
2038